North American Historical Atlases

THE CIVIL WAR:
1861-1863

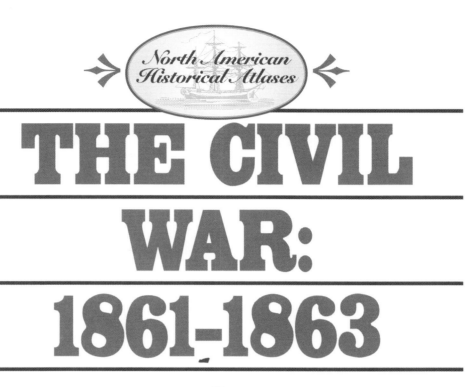

North American Historical Atlases

THE CIVIL WAR: 1861-1863

Rebecca Stefoff

BENCHMARK BOOKS

MARSHALL CAVENDISH
NEW YORK

Benchmark Books
Marshall Cavendish Corporation
99 White Plains Road
Tarrytown, New York 10591
www.marshallcavendish.com

• • •

Library of Congress Cataloging-in-Publication Data
Stefoff, Rebecca, 1951-
The Civil War: 1861–1863/by Rebecca Stefoff
p. cm—(North American historical atlases)
Includes bibliographical references and index.
Summary: Presents information on some of the causes of the Civil War, the battles fought between
1861 and 1863, and the signing of the Emancipation Proclamation.
ISBN 0-7614-1346-4 (lib.bdg.)
1. United States—History—Civil War, 1861–1865—Juvenile literature.   2. United States—History—Civil War, 1861–1865—Maps—Juvenile literature.
[1. United States—History—Civil War, 1861–1865.   2. United States—History—Civil War, 1861–1865—Maps.   I. Title.
E468 .S84   2002   2002043768   973. 7—dc21

• • •

Printed in Hong Kong
6 5 4 3 2 1

• • •

Book Designer: Judith Turziano
Photo Researcher: Candlepants, Inc.

• • •

Contents

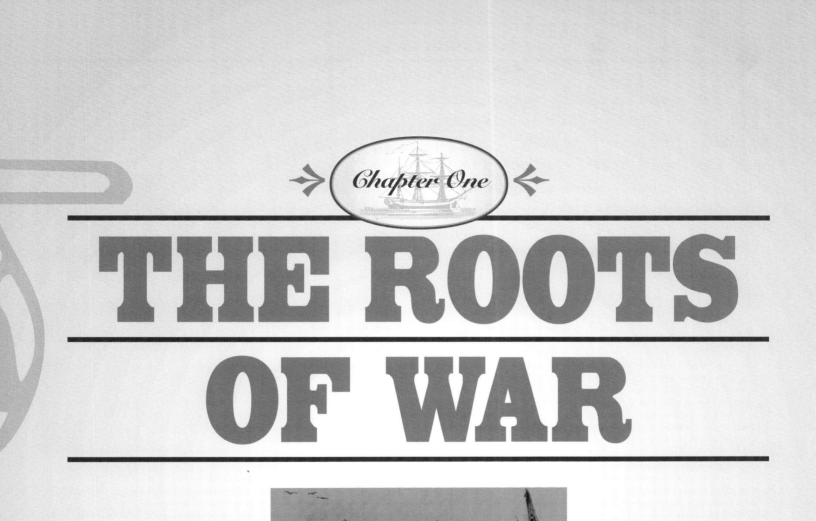

Chapter One

THE ROOTS OF WAR

A civil war turns a nation against itself. In the middle of the nineteenth century, the American Civil War nearly tore apart the United States. It killed more than 600,000 soldiers, overthrew a way of life, and pitted family members and neighbors against each other in battles larger and more horrifying than Americans had ever seen. The first shots were fired in 1861, after conflicts between the Northern and Southern parts of the country had brewed for years.

The Problem of Slavery

The Civil War happened because the Southern states wanted to break away from the United States to form a new, independent country. Northern leaders, determined to keep the United States united, would not let them go.

Slavery was the biggest cause of the bitter split between North and South. From the earliest days of settlement in the Americas, landowners in warm Southern regions had used slave labor on **plantations** to grow tobacco, sugar, and cotton for the world market. Supplying the Americas with enslaved men, women, and children from Africa became big business, but slavery did not take root everywhere.

The Northern United States developed an economy based on trade, manufacturing, and small farming. During the eighteenth century, the Northern states outlawed slavery, partly because it was economically unnecessary and

A family of African-American slaves picks cotton on a plantation near Savannah, Georgia. Slavery was not the only cause of the Civil War, but it was a major contributing factor.

partly because of the rise of the **abolition** movement, which called slavery unjust and immoral.

The economy of the South was firmly based on plantation agriculture and the slavery that made it possible. By the nineteenth century, about a third of all Southerners owned slaves. Only about 40,000 slaveholders owned 20 or more slaves, but those big plantation owners controlled virtually all of the South's wealth and agricultural land, and they set the pattern

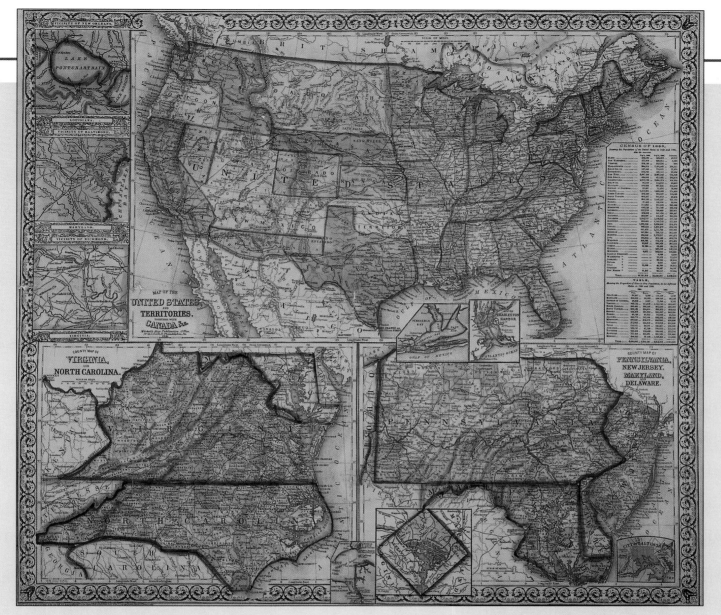

Philadelphia mapmaker Samuel A. Mitchell published this excellent map of the United States in 1849, just a few years before the outbreak of the Civil War. California and the Southwest are still shown as part of Mexico, although they had become U.S. territories a year earlier.

for the region's culture. Northern **abolitionists** passionately wanted to end Southern slavery, but there were some Northerners who profited through Southern trade and wanted slavery to

"WE MUST AND SHALL BE FREE"

Abolitionists were a minority everywhere, but they made themselves heard. One of the most forceful was a free African American named David Walker. In 1829, he published a booklet called the *Appeal* urging his fellow blacks to rise up and claim their freedom, by force if necessary. "Never make an attempt to gain our freedom or natural rights from under our cruel oppressors and murderers until you see your way clear—when that hour arrives and you move, be not afraid or dismayed," Walker wrote. "They have no more right to hold us in slavery than we have to hold them...." He continued, "America is more our country than it is the whites'—we have enriched it with our blood and tears.... I speak Americans for your good. We must and shall be free I say, in spite of you.... And woe, woe, will be to you if we have to obtain our freedom by fighting." White readers did not miss the warning in Walker's words. David Walker's *Appeal* fueled Southern fears of a slave uprising and led to stricter laws for free and slave blacks.

continue. And other Northerners did not care about the issue at all. The South had a few abolitionists, but most Southerners defended slavery. Above all, they wanted to do things their own way, free from Northern interference.

Violence in the West

The widening split over slavery became a crisis when new states joined the nation. In 1819, the country had eleven states that permitted slavery and eleven that did not. Slave states and free states were politically balanced. Then the Missouri Territory asked to become a state. Northerners wanted Missouri to be a free state.

They were afraid that if the U.S. Senate had more members from slave states than from free states, the South would gain too much power over the national government. Southerners, of course, wanted Missouri to become a slave state for exactly that reason.

After much heated argument, Congress found a solution. It made Missouri a slave state and created the free state of Maine, originally part of Massachusetts. It also banned slavery from all new territory north of Missouri's southern boundary. This decision, the Missouri Compromise of 1820, kept the balance and the peace—but the underlying problem did not go away.

Gun battles, ambushes, and raids by both antislavery and proslavery groups turned Kansas into a bloody war zone. Each side committed violent crimes to further what it saw as its all-important cause.

During the 1840s, the United States prepared to create more states from western territories. Some Southerners feared that new free states would tip the balance of Senate power to the North. A few began saying that the South should **secede** from the United States and go its own way. Disturbed by such talk, Congress again struggled to reach a solution. The Compromise of 1850 made California a free state but allowed slavery in the territories of

For years before the Civil War, the nation's leaders struggled to keep the tension between slave and free states from splitting the country apart. The key was keeping the number of states—and therefore the number of senators in Congress—on both sides equal. Trouble arose over the question of creating new states from the western territories. Would the new states be slave or free? The Compromise of 1850 and the Kansas-Nebraska Act were attempts to preserve the delicate balance and determine the future of the territories. Tragically, they failed to satisfy either side.

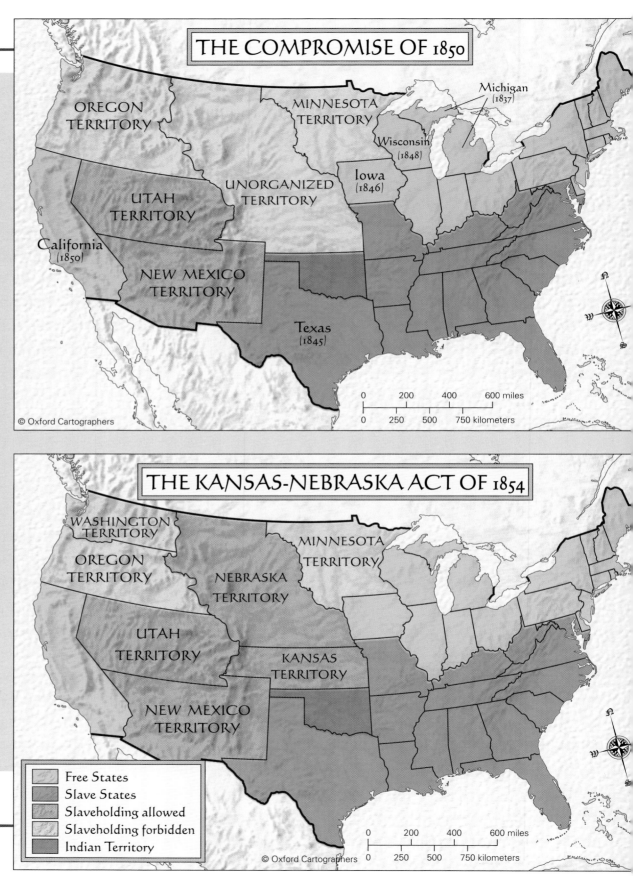

THE COMPROMISE OF 1850

OREGON TERRITORY

MINNESOTA TERRITORY

Michigan (1837)

Wisconsin (1848)

UTAH TERRITORY

UNORGANIZED TERRITORY

Iowa (1846)

California (1850)

NEW MEXICO TERRITORY

Texas (1845)

© Oxford Cartographers

| 0 | 200 | 400 | 600 miles |
| 0 | 250 | 500 | 750 kilometers |

THE KANSAS-NEBRASKA ACT OF 1854

WASHINGTON TERRITORY

MINNESOTA TERRITORY

OREGON TERRITORY

NEBRASKA TERRITORY

UTAH TERRITORY

KANSAS TERRITORY

NEW MEXICO TERRITORY

Free States
Slave States
Slaveholding allowed
Slaveholding forbidden
Indian Territory

© Oxford Cartographers

| 0 | 200 | 400 | 600 miles |
| 0 | 250 | 500 | 750 kilometers |

New Mexico (now New Mexico and Arizona) and Utah. Congress also passed the Fugitive Slave Act, which made it easier for slaveowners to capture runaway slaves and ordered punishment for anyone who helped the runaways. President Millard Fillmore called the Compromise of 1850 the "final settlement" of the slavery issue. Unfortunately, he was wrong.

Four years later, Congress passed the Kansas-Nebraska Act, which let settlers in the territories vote on whether their states would be slave or free. The act enraged abolitionists, who feared it would allow slavery in places where the Missouri Compromise had banned it. With Kansas on the verge of statehood, abolitionists and supporters of slavery stormed into the territory, each side seeking to win control. A proslavery government was elected, but abolitionists elected a rival government. Armed attacks by both sides turned the state into a battleground called Bleeding Kansas. Around the same time, some Northerners formed a new political party, the Republicans, dedicated to keeping slavery—and Southern power—from spreading.

The Supreme Court Fans the Flames

The Fugitive Slave Act was unpopular in the North because it let African Americans be seized in free states and carried back into slavery. In 1857, enemies of slavery were even

Dred Scott took his quest for freedom all the way to the U.S. Supreme Court, which rejected his claim and ruled that he was property, not a person. The decision fueled the fires of abolitionism across the North.

more outraged when the U.S. Supreme Court decided the fate of an African-American man named Dred Scott.

Scott was a slave from Missouri who had lived

A SHOWDOWN IN BOSTON

 The sufferings of African Americans during the 1850s won support for the abolitionist cause. In 1854 Anthony Burns, an escaped slave from Virginia, was imprisoned in Boston, a hotbed of abolitionism. While Burns was waiting to be returned to his owner, abolitionists stormed the **federal** courthouse where he was held. They killed a law officer but failed to liberate Burns. They also failed in an attempt to buy Burns's freedom, and they watched in anger and despair as he was carried back to slavery. Eventually, Boston's abolitionists succeeded in buying freedom for Burns. The abolitionists also helped him get a college education, and he later became a minister. Abolitionists also inspired Boston to pass local laws making it harder to enforce the Fugitive Slave Act.

In the 1850s, abolitionists wait outside a Boston courthouse where a case involving an escaped slave is being heard. Outraged that black fugitives could be seized in free states and carried back into slavery, Boston's abolitionists frequently ignored laws that enforced slavery.

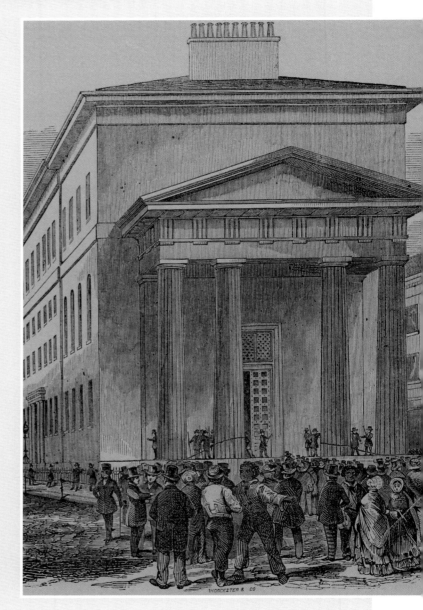

with his owner in Illinois and Wisconsin before being taken back to Missouri. Aided by abolitionist lawyers, Scott sued for his freedom, claiming that he could no longer be a slave because he had lived in places that did not allow slavery. His case went to the Supreme Court, which ruled that Scott was still a slave and should not even have been allowed to sue because he was property, not a citizen. Then the Court went further and declared that the Missouri Compromise of 1820 was unconstitutional because Congress had no power to outlaw slavery anywhere.

Not surprisingly, the outcome of the *Dred Scott* case thrilled the South. In the North, horrified Republicans and abolitionists vowed to overturn the decision. The affair aroused so much righteous fury that black abolitionist leader Frederick Douglass hoped that case would somehow lead to "a complete overthrow of the whole slave system." Douglass's hopes were fulfilled, in a way. The case was one of many events that led up to the Civil War and, eventually, the end of slavery.

A House Divided

In 1858, the race for a U.S. Senate seat from Illinois highlighted the nation's tense mood and the gap between slave and free states. The candidates were Democrat Stephen A. Douglas, who disapproved of slavery but felt that the issue should be settled by each

Abraham Lincoln (white jacket) debated Stephen A. Douglas (behind him) during their campaign for a U.S. Senate seat from Illinois. Slavery was one of their chief topics. Lincoln opposed slavery, not only on moral grounds, but also because he feared it would cause a political crisis within the United States.

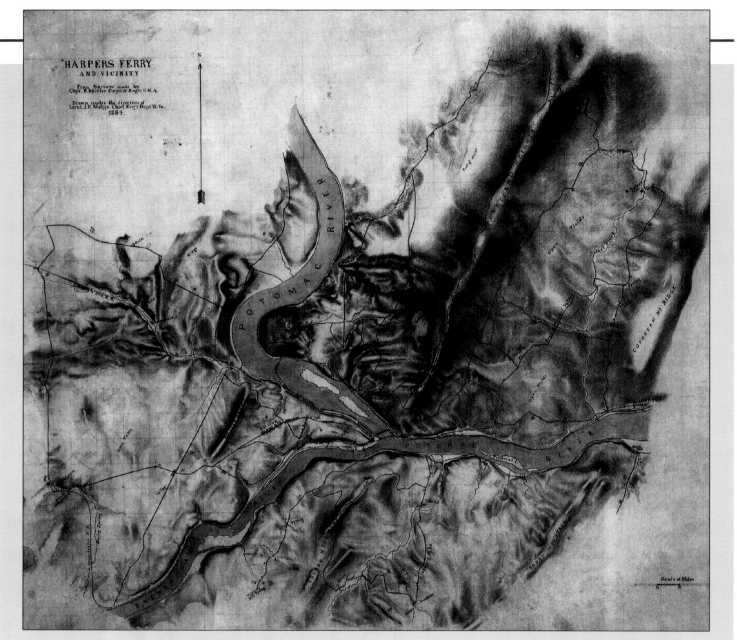

Harper's Ferry, Virginia, was the site of a botched abolitionist raid in 1859. Here it appears in an 1864 map by Union officer J.R. Meigs. Based on an earlier army survey, the map shows such details as a pontoon bridge across the Potomac River. Soon after making this map, Meigs died in action while serving as engineer on the staff of Philip Sheridan, a Union general.

territory's voters, and Republican Abraham Lincoln, who disapproved of slavery and thought it should not be allowed to spread. In a speech accepting his party's nomination to run for the Senate, Lincoln had spoken these memorable words, echoing the Bible:

A house divided against itself cannot stand. I believe that this Government cannot endure permanently half slave and half free.

The two men exchanged views at a series of seven political debates in Illinois. Although Lincoln stated plainly that he and the Republican Party thought slavery was wrong, he saw that the rift between North and South threatened to crack the country wide open. His greatest concern was not ending slavery but preserving the United States. The best way to do this, Lincoln thought, was not to attack the slave system in the South but to limit the spread of slavery and wait for time to erode it. He was more patient than abolitionists like John Brown, who had killed slaveowners in Kansas. In 1859, Brown led a disastrous raid on Harpers Ferry, Virginia, hoping to start a slave rebellion. Brown thought God had chosen him to free the slaves, but he was captured and hanged for murder and treason. His plot convinced Southerners that the North planned to attack slavery not just in the new territories but also in the South itself.

Although Douglas won the senatorial election of 1858, Lincoln had attracted national attention, and the Republican Party chose him as its candidate for president in 1860. Slavery was the main issue of the election, and simple math decided the outcome. The North had 71 percent of the country's people. The South had 29 percent, a third of them slaves who could not vote. The election went to Lincoln, who won the entire North. After the results were announced, Lincoln's comment to the newspaper reporters was, "Well, boys, your troubles are over now. Mine have just begun."

Secession!

A few weeks after Lincoln's victory, South Carolina's state government voted to secede. It declared that "the union now subsisting between South Carolina and other States under the name of the United States of America is hereby dissolved." South Carolina's **secession** was no surprise—its leaders had always claimed that individual states had more right to govern themselves than the federal government had to control them. Secession put this belief in states' rights to the ultimate test.

South Carolina did not stand alone for long. By February 1861, Texas, Louisiana, Mississippi, Alabama, Florida, and Georgia had also seceded. The secessionists created a new national government they called the Confederate States of America, electing Senator Jefferson Davis of Mississippi as their president. Virginia, North Carolina, Tennessee,

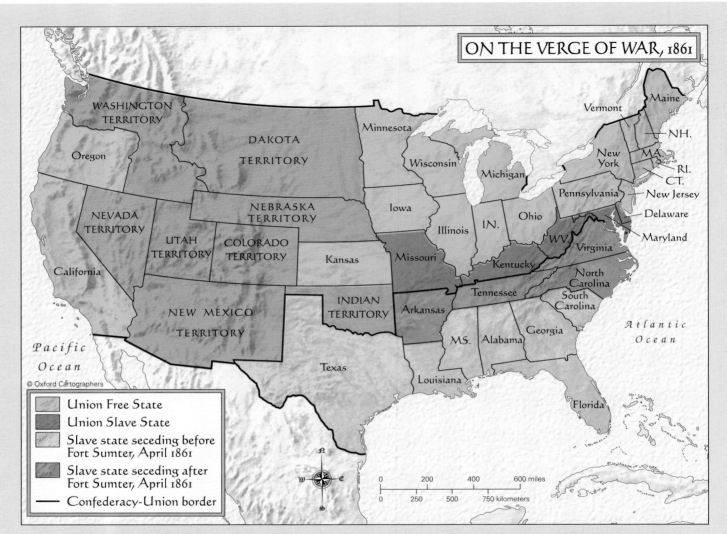

WASHINGTON TERRITORY

Oregon

DAKOTA TERRITORY

Minnesota

Vermont

Maine

NH.

Wisconsin

Michigan

New York

MA.

RI.

CT.

New Jersey

NEVADA TERRITORY

NEBRASKA TERRITORY

Iowa

Pennsylvania

Delaware

UTAH TERRITORY

COLORADO TERRITORY

Illinois

IN.

Ohio

W.V.

Maryland

California

Kansas

Missouri

Kentucky

Virginia

New Mexico Territory

Indian Territory

Arkansas

Tennessee

North Carolina

South Carolina

Pacific Ocean

Texas

MS.

Alabama

Georgia

Atlantic Ocean

© Oxford Cartographers

Louisiana

Florida

Union Free State

Union Slave State

Slave state seceding before Fort Sumter, April 1861

Slave state seceding after Fort Sumter, April 1861

Confederacy-Union border

0   200   400   600 miles

0   250   500   750 kilometers

After Lincoln was elected president, seven Southern states left the Union. Their representatives met in Alabama to declare the independence of the Confederate States of America. After fighting began with the attack on Fort Sumter, four more states joined the Confederacy. The slave states of Delaware, Maryland, Kentucky, and Missouri stayed in the Union, as did the western part of Virginia (although it was not recognized as the separate state of West Virginia until 1863). These "border states" played a key role in the war. They were a buffer zone between Confederate forces and the capital and heartland of the Union. They also endured some of the fiercest fighting, divided loyalties and conflicts within families and communities, and great destruction of homes and property.

and Arkansas would soon join the Confederacy.

Many Southerners felt wild excitement over what a women's club in Georgia called "the fearless and heroic act" of secession. Others realized the seriousness of the matter. Robert E. Lee of Virginia, who would become the commander of the Confederate army, wrote, "I see only that a fearful calamity is upon us." In the North, some abolitionists welcomed secession because it would create a United States free of slavery. A Republican newspaper urged that the secessionists be allowed to "depart in peace." But Lincoln probably spoke for the majority of Northerners when he argued that the federal government's authority was stronger than states' rights and that "no state... can lawfully get out of the Union." Now that he was president, what would he do about it?

Chapter Two

NORTH AGAINST SOUTH

In his **inaugural** speech on March 4, 1861, Lincoln spoke to the South that had seceded as well as to the North that had elected him. After repeating an earlier promise not to interfere with slavery where it already existed, Lincoln announced that he would "defend and maintain" the Union "in all the States." He also said to the South, "You can have no conflict without being yourselves the aggressors." In other words, Lincoln warned of civil war but said that the North would not fire a shot unless the South fired first. Would the South turn

When sworn into office as the nation's sixteenth president, Abraham Lincoln knew that the country was on the verge of breaking apart. No president has ever borne a greater burden in office than Lincoln, who occupied the White House during the nation's only civil war.

away from war? Soon he—and the nation—would know the answer.

The Fall of Fort Sumter

Lincoln was determined to hang on to federal property in the South. On his first day in office, he learned that a federal fort on an island in the harbor of Charleston, South Carolina, was almost out of supplies. He warned the governor of South Carolina that he was shipping supplies to Fort Sumter and waited to see what the South would do.

The Confederates ordered the fort to surrender. Its commander refused. Hoping to capture Fort Sumter before the supplies arrived, Jefferson Davis ordered Confederate forces to begin firing cannons at it on April 12, 1861. The soldiers inside the fort fired back, but after thirty-three hours of exchanging fire, their stone walls were crumbling. They could not hold out much longer. Fort Sumter surrendered on April 14, and both sides knew that the war had begun. No one on either side had been badly wounded or killed—but no one could begin to imagine how many would perish in the battles to come.

The North

The North, or Union, had several advantages over the South. One was sheer population size: more than 20 million Northerners to 9 million Southerners (about 3.5 million of them slaves).

Another advantage was that the four slave states of Maryland, Kentucky, Missouri, and Delaware stayed with the Union instead of seceding. Part of Virginia even rejoined the Union—Congress made it into a separate free state called West Virginia. These border states saw fierce fighting between neighbors who supported rival sides, but overall they remained true to the Union. They provided a buffer between the South and the industrial centers of the North.

Industry was a key Northern advantage. With most of the country's factories, the Union had more guns, ammunition, uniforms, boots, and other war gear than the South. It also had most of the country's railroad cars and nearly three-quarters of its railway track, and it could move soldiers and supplies more easily than the South. The Union controlled most of the national navy, giving it an advantage at sea.

But the Union faced some significant disadvantages, too. Its capital, Washington, D.C., was dangerously close to Confederate territory (and would have been inside Confederate territory if Maryland had seceded). At the beginning of the war, its army numbered only around 16,000 men, spread across a wide area. The Union's first task was to **recruit** and train new soldiers. By midsummer of 1861, about 200,000 men were enlisted. Many people in the North opposed the war, however, and eventually men refusing to serve in the army led riots in several cities.

Lincoln and the other Union leaders knew that if they had to fight deep in the South, in unfamiliar territory where people strongly supported the Confederate cause, winning the war would be difficult. Instead they hoped to win quickly with a three-part plan: closing Southern ports with a **blockade** to keep the South from getting supplies from Europe or selling its cotton; controlling the Mississippi River to cut the Confederacy in two and keep Southerners from using the river as a supply line; and capturing Richmond, Virginia, the Confederate capital.

Union sailors fire on a Confederate blockade runner as it flees into a rainstorm. The North's blockade failed to keep daring blockade runners from bringing much-needed goods into the South.

Dreams of military glory collided with the grim realities of war on July 21, 1861, when Union and Confederate forces clashed at the First Battle of Bull Run (sometimes called Manassas in the South).

The South

The South's chief advantage was the loyalty that most white Southerners felt to the Confederacy. They were fighting not just for an idea or a way of life but for their homes, their families, and their very soil—much like the American colonies when they rebelled against Great Britain in the Revolutionary War. The South also had a number of gifted military officers. By midsummer of 1861, about 112,000 men were serving in the Confederate army.

Unlike the North, the South had no need or desire to occupy enemy territory. The Confederacy's goal was to have its independence recognized by the United States and other nations. Southerners hoped that Great Britain and France, the biggest buyers of Southern cotton, would recognize the Confederacy and urge the Union to make peace. The South's plan was to defend its territory fiercely and wear out the North. If Southern generals got a chance to advance into Union territory, they would do so to frighten and discourage the Northern population.

The Hardest Battle Ever Fought

For ten weeks after the fall of Fort Sumter, the war hardly seemed real. Both sides made plans, rushed new recruits through training, and

Léon J. Frémeaux of New Orleans, a captain of engineers in the Confederate army, drew this sketch map of the First Battle of Manassas or Bull Run. Troops led by Captain F. B. Schaeffer are positioned in the forest across from the cornfield. The drawing at the bottom shows that the Confederate troops (shown on the right bank of the stream) had an advantage over the Union troops on the opposite side, because they could fire down upon them.

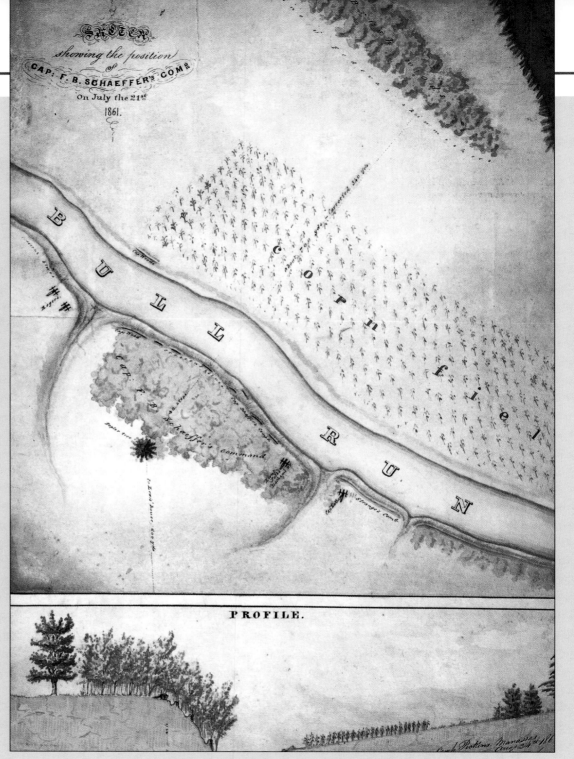

slowly moved their forces into position. The North sent troops toward Richmond, and the South sent troops to block the way.

On the blistering day of July 21, 1861, the two armies met near a shallow creek called Bull Run near Manassas, Virginia. The 35,000 Union soldiers, called Yankees or Yanks by their opponents, wore blue uniforms. The Confederate soldiers, known to the Northerners as Rebels or Rebs, numbered about 20,000 and were clad in gray. The great majority on both sides had never seen battle before. Neither had the audience. Picnickers had come in carriages from Washington, less than thirty miles away, to watch their troops teach the Rebs a lesson. The day provided plenty of excitement, but not the kind they had expected.

Amid heat, dust, and confusion, the two armies met and began firing. At first it seemed that victory would go to the Union. Then a Southern general named Thomas Jackson led a volunteer force into the battle and held his position "like a stone wall," as a fellow Southern officer admiringly said, earning him the nickname Stonewall Jackson. Just then, 11,000 Confederate troops arrived by train and revived the South's fading strength. The Rebel

General Thomas Jackson of the Confederate army won the nickname Stonewall for his firm stand at First Bull Run. Officers and soldiers on both sides admired Jackson's bravery and his cool-headed, clever leadership.

An injured and sick soldier is comforted by a comrade. Despite the best efforts of doctors and nurses, medical facilities during the Civil War were severely limited. More men on both sides died of disease and infected wounds than were killed outright on the battlefields.

The Civil War: 1861–1863

TO FIGHT OR NOT TO FIGHT

In the first exciting weeks after Fort Sumter, young men on both sides ran to enlist in the army, eager to see action before the fighting was over. War seemed like a grand, noble adventure. But all too soon those young men met the grim realities of terror, pain, and death. After the First Battle of Bull Run, New Hampshire soldier George Sargent wrote to his brother: "If you have not enlisted, don't you do it. If you do, you will wish you had not. Now don't you do it and if you have enlisted, get out of it as soon as you can." Such letters, along with newspaper reports of deaths, cooled the enthusiasm, and voluntary enlistments fell on both sides. In the spring of 1862, the Confederacy had to pass a draft law that required men to be available for military service. The Union did the same in the spring of 1863.

Many of those who fought in the Civil War, like this Union soldier from Michigan's 4th Infantry, were young men, often teenagers.

force surged forward. The Yankees fell back in dismay, then retreated in panic. Blue-clad soldiers flung aside their guns and ran for their lives, knocking down terrified onlookers. At day's end, the Confederacy claimed victory. More than 600 men had died on each side— more than in any other battle in the United States up to that time. It was, reported Union soldier George Sargent, in a letter to his brother, "the hardest Battle ever fought in this Country." Suddenly the war had become not only real but bloody.

*Two ironclad ships—the Union **Monitor** and the Confederate **Merrimack** or **Virginia**—fought a showy but not very important battle off Virginia. Northern leaders had feared that the Confederacy would use its ironclad to destroy the Union navy, but in the end the South sank the **Merrimack** to keep it out of Union hands.*

The War at Sea

The South's coastline was 3,500 miles long (5,600 kilometers), much of it fringed with swamps and islands where boats could hide. The Union navy never managed to blockade the entire coast, and smugglers called blockade-runners brought some supplies into the South. Still, the blockade created Southern shortages of imported goods such as shoes, nails, guns, and bullets. In the summer and fall of 1861, Union gunboats also destroyed or captured several Confederate forts and ports along the Carolina coast.

The most famous naval battle of the war took place at Hampton Roads, off the Virginia coast, on March 9, 1862. The Confederates had

The Union fleet lies anchored in the Mississippi River at New Orleans. Leading the capture of the Confederacy's key port was David Farragut, a Southerner who stayed loyal to the Union and served in its navy. His victory at New Orleans closed the river to Confederate trade and cut off a route for the sale of Southern cotton.

salvaged an abandoned Union ship called the *Merrimack* and covered it with iron plates for protection against **artillery** shells. The Confederates renamed it the *Virginia* and used it to attack and sink some Northern ships, whose guns could not hurt it. The Union, meanwhile, had built an ironclad ship of its own, the *Monitor,* which it sent to battle the *Virginia.* The two ships bombarded each other to a stalemate—neither could harm the other. The Confederates destroyed their ironclad so that the Union could not get it, and the *Monitor* sank in a storm. Although the *Virginia* and the *Monitor* had little real effect on the war, they ushered in a new age of metal-clad ships.

The following month, on April 25, the Union won a major naval victory. A fleet of battleships captured the wealthy Confederate port city of New Orleans, Louisiana. This gave the Union control of much of the Mississippi River, which Northern leaders considered vital to winning the war.

Chapter Three

TO SAVE
THE UNION

During the winter of 1861–1862, the Northern and Southern armies trained, planned, and maneuvered in preparation for future clashes. When spring came, they stirred into action in a string of battles that failed to give a clear advantage to either side.

The War in the West

Early in the Civil War, important conflicts took place near the Mississippi River. In February 1862, Union forces led by General Ulysses S. Grant captured Forts Henry and Donelson from the Confederates in northern Tennessee. After Grant demanded "immediate and unconditional surrender" of the forts, some of his soldiers began calling him Unconditional Surrender Grant, a play on his initials.

Grant then led a 40,000-man army south through Tennessee. On the morning of April 6, the army was camped near the old Shiloh Church at Pittsburgh Landing when Confederate forces attacked. Caught cooking breakfast, the Yankees scrambled for their weapons. They managed to kill one of the Confederate generals and hold off the Rebels until Union reinforcements arrived. The battle continued the next day. By the time the Confederates retreated, about 23,000 men had been killed or wounded, and the Union army claimed about the same number of casualties. People were shocked by the savagery and suffering of Shiloh.

Union officer Ulysses S. Grant distinguished himself in several western campaigns early in the war. His capture of two Confederate forts interrupted Southern army communication on the Memphis and Ohio railway line, which passed near the forts.

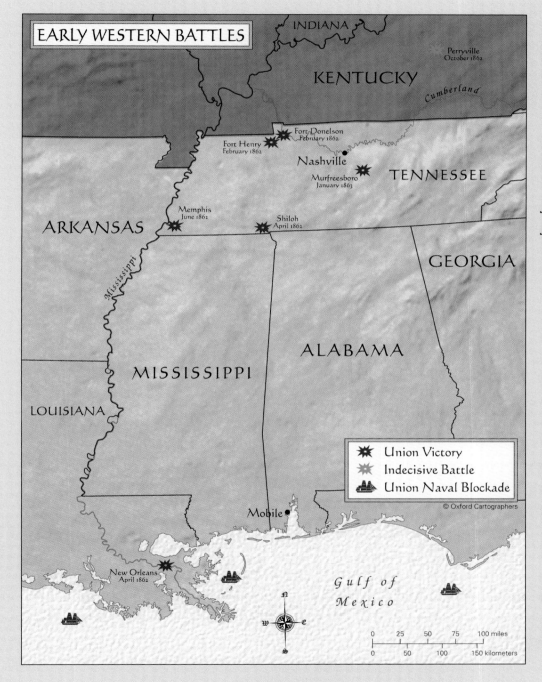

EARLY WESTERN BATTLES

INDIANA

KENTUCKY

Perryville
October 1862

Cumberland

Fort Donelson
February 1862

Fort Henry
February 1862

Nashville

Murfreesboro
January 1863

TENNESSEE

Memphis
June 1862

Shiloh
April 1862

ARKANSAS

GEORGIA

ALABAMA

MISSISSIPPI

LOUISIANA

Union Victory
Indecisive Battle
Union Naval Blockade

© Oxford Cartographers

Mobile

New Orleans
April 1862

Gulf of
Mexico

0   25   50   75   100 miles

0   50   100   150 kilometers

Mississippi

The war in the west centered on the Mississippi River. Early in the conflict, both sides hoped to gain control of this vital waterway. At first, Confederate forces outnumbered Union troops in the region. But in early 1862, several Union armies moved into the area. A series of Union victories in western Tennessee, together with the capture of New Orleans, ended Confederate dreams of holding on to the Mississippi. For the rest of the war, the Confederacy was hemmed in by enemies on its western, as well as its northern, frontier.

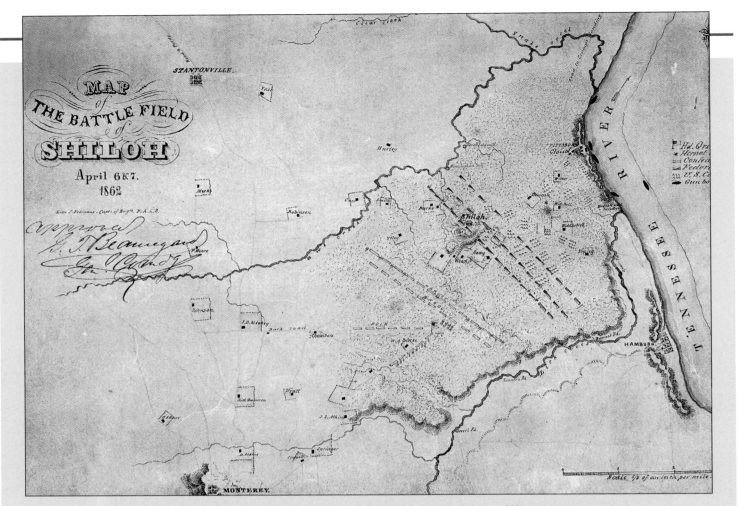

Frémeaux also produced this map of Shiloh, probably to illustrate a report by P. T. G. Beauregard, a Southern general. Unlike many mapmakers and engineers on the Southern side, Frémeaux survived the war to return to his home in New Orleans and his hobby of watercolor painting.

Changing Fortunes

General George B. McClellan was Lincoln's first chief commander of the Union forces. He would not be the last—Lincoln had a hard time finding a commander who would carry on the war the way the president wanted. Lincoln was in favor of moving against Confederate troops outside Washington, but McClellan did not agree. Instead, he moved the Union army south in early 1862 in an attempt to capture Richmond. Confederate forces, commanded by General Robert E. Lee, drove the Yankees back in a series of battles. A few weeks earlier, Stonewall Jackson had successfully defended a Union invasion of Virginia's Shenandoah Valley, beating the Bluecoats in a dozen battles. The North's attempt to seize Southern strongholds was a dismal failure.

To make matters worse, Jackson led a daring raid on Union field headquarters and captured a large sum of money and the uniform of one of the Northern generals. Humiliation was

In the first two years of the war, the Union army employed civilian balloonists to rise high into the air in balloons to spy out enemy positions and movements. Most Union officers scorned the work of the Balloon Corps. One complained that, "They always see lions in our path." Still, the balloonists made many useful reports. Drawings and maps such as this one were rare, however, because the balloons moved so much that even trained artists found it hard to draw.

President Lincoln (center) visits the camp of General George B. McClellan (right), commander of the Army of the Potomac. On the left stands Major Allen Allan Pinkerton, a famous detective who served as Lincoln's bodyguard. During the war, detectives employed by Pinkerton acted as spies and messengers for the Union.

soon followed by defeat. In late August, the two sides met a second time at Bull Run, Virginia (called Second Manassas in the South), and a second time the South soundly defeated the North. Now Northerners feared that the victorious Confederate soldiers might invade their own capital, Washington, D.C.

Antietam

Hoping to carry the war into Northern territory, Lee ordered his forces into Maryland. Forty thousand Confederate troops were spread through the cornfields and woods along Antietam Creek near Sharpsburg when McClellan's 75,000-man army swooped down on them on September 17. In hard combat, the Northern troops beat Lee and his men back, forcing them to retreat into Virginia. A Wisconsin soldier later recalled,

> *Another line of our men came up through the corn. We all joined together, jumped over the fence, and again pushed out into the open field.... 'Forward' is the word. The men are loading and firing with demoniacal fury and shouting and laughing hysterically, and the whole field before us is covered with rebels fleeing for life, into the woods.*

With more than 5,000 killed and nearly 20,000 wounded, the Battle of Antietam marked the deadliest day in a bloody war. Casualties were fairly equal, but the battle was considered a Union victory—although scarcely

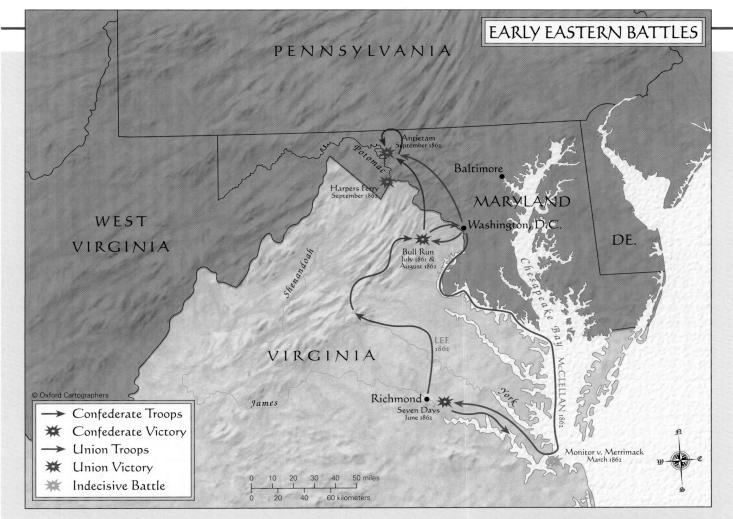

PENNSYLVANIA

WEST VIRGINIA

Antietam
September 1862

Harpers Ferry
September 1862

Baltimore

MARYLAND

Washington, D.C.

DE.

Bull Run
July 1861 &
August 1862

Potomac

Shenandoah

VIRGINIA

LEE
1862

Chesapeake Bay

McCLELLAN 1862

© Oxford Cartographers

James

Richmond
Seven Days
June 1862

York

Monitor v. Merrimack
March 1862

→ Confederate Troops
✳ Confederate Victory
→ Union Troops
✳ Union Victory
✳ Indecisive Battle

0 10 20 30 40 50 miles
0   20   40   60 kilometers

No clear winner or loser emerged from the battles in the east during the early years
of the war. McClellan's Army of the Potomac tried to capture the Confederate capital of
Richmond, Virginia. Union troops got close to the city, but were driven back in a series
of clashes called the Seven Days. The Confederates then defeated Union forces—for a
second time—at Bull Run or Manassas. This left a victorious Confederate army under
Robert E. Lee just twenty miles from Washington. Now it seemed that the Union
capital might fall to the enemy. Instead, Lee advanced boldly into Maryland, but after
a terrible day of slaughter at Antietam, survivors of his army slipped back into
Virginia. After many bloody, desperate clashes, neither side had gained a real advantage.

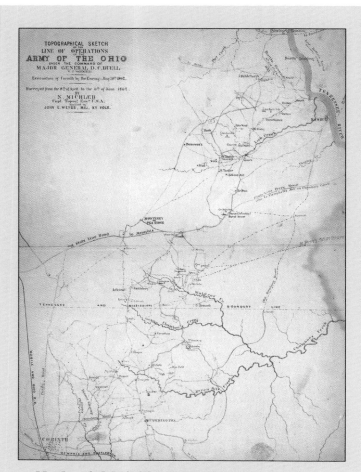

Nathaniel Michler and his assistant, John Weyss, accompanied the Union army of General Henry B.W. Halleck from Tennessee to Corinth, Mississippi (lower left). They made this map, showing many details of the march. Michler and Weyss achieved great recognition as Union mapmakers, and after the war the army assigned them to survey and map a number of eastern battlefields.

a glorious triumph for McClellan. Lincoln expected McClellan to follow Lee's defeated troops and smash the Rebel army. When McClellan failed to do so, Lincoln replaced him with General Ambrose Burnside.

Emancipation

Around the time of the Second Battle of Bull Run, Lincoln spelled out his war goals in a letter to the *New York Tribune.* "My paramount object in this struggle is to save the Union, and is not either to save or to destroy slavery," he wrote. "If I could save the Union without freeing any slave, I would do it, and if I could save it by freeing all the slaves, I would do it; and if I could save it by freeing some and leaving others alone I would also do that." But after the Battle of Antietam, with Northern spirits rising and the South feeling the sting of defeat, Lincoln decided the time had come to address the fate of the slaves.

The president had been wanting for some time to emancipate, or free, the slaves, even at the risk of angering the slave states along the border that had remained loyal to the Union. Emancipation was not simply a **humanitarian** act—Lincoln and other Northern leaders believed that slave labor was helping the Confederacy survive. Many African Americans had already deserted the South to help the Union cause, and Lincoln expected that news of emancipation would encourage more of

BAD LUCK FOR LEE

Robert E. Lee (center), photographed after the war with his son, General George Washington Custis Lee (right), and an aide (left).

If not for some very bad luck, the South might have avoided the colossal conflict at Antietam, and the war might have ended differently. Four days before the battle, Union forces in Maryland camped where Confederate forces had been a day or so earlier. Soldier Barton Mitchell spied a small package lying in a patch of clover. It contained three cigars wrapped in a handwritten document that was signed by the assistant to General Robert E. Lee, commander of the Confederate forces, and addressed to Lee's generals. Realizing that he had stumbled onto something big, Mitchell gave the paper to an officer, and eventually it reached Union commander George B. McClellan (no one knows what happened to the cigars). The document was Lee's plan for an advance into Northern territory, with orders telling each part of Lee's army where to go. McClellan could have used this knowledge to wipe out the separate Confederate divisions, but he was too timid for such a bold step. By the time he made up his mind to act, the divisions had formed a single large force. Still, the lost order allowed McClellan to catch up with Lee at Antietam and keep him from moving northward. Some historians think that if Mitchell had not found Lee's lost order, the South might have marched to victories in Maryland and Pennsylvania. If so, France and Great Britain might have pressured the Union to make peace with the Confederacy. Lee's chance to make this happen vanished because a careless Southern officer left a top-secret order behind.

Lincoln reads a draft of the Emancipation Proclamation to his cabinet of advisors. The proclamation officially freed the Southern slaves, but black Americans in the Confederacy would not be truly free unless and until the North won the war.

them to abandon the South's fields, workshops, and dockyards.

Five days after Antietam, Lincoln promised to declare the slaves free on January 1, 1863. Blacks in the South and the North, slave and free, began planning for what they called the Day of Jubilee. A group of African Americans in New Orleans, for example, asked the Union general there for permission to hold a parade past Union headquarters, followed by a grand dinner to celebrate their freedom and to raise funds for needy black women and children. At the same time, Southern whites dreaded what they feared would be a bloody slave uprising on the day of emancipation.

On the appointed day, Lincoln signed into law the Emancipation Proclamation, which said that "all persons held as slaves within any State...in rebellion against the United States, shall be...forever free." The proclamation did not apply to the border states, and the Union could not enforce it in Confederate territory, so it had little real effect on the lives of most slaves. But its meaning was unmistakable—if the North won the war, slavery was doomed. All Americans, Northern or Southern, black or white, knew that they had reached a historic turning point. And by this time they also knew that the war that had been expected to end so quickly was very far from over

Glossary

abolition: the act of doing away with or ending something, usually used to refer to the movement to end slavery

abolitionist: one who works to abolish, or end, slavery

artillery: large guns used in warfare, such as cannons

blockade: barrier to control or eliminate traffic; at sea, usually a line of ships to keep enemy vessels from entering or leaving ports

federal: relating to the national government

humanitarian: based on ideas or beliefs about the need to treat other human beings with kindness, fairness, and generosity

inaugural: relating to an inauguration, the formal start of a term of office

plantation: large farm devoted to production of a single crop, usually for sale rather than for local use

recruit: to draw in a new member; someone who has recently joined a group

salvage: to reclaim or rescue something that has been discarded or sunk

secede: to formally leave or withdraw

secession: act of seceding, or formally withdrawing, from a union or group

Further Reading

Catton, Bruce. *The American Heritage New History of the Civil War.* New York: Viking, 1996.

——. *This Hallowed Ground: The Story of the Union Side of the Civil War.* Garden City, NY: Doubleday, 1962.

Clinton, Catherine. *Scholastic Encyclopedia of the Civil War.* New York: Scholastic Reference, 1999.

Dolan, Edward. *The American Civil War: A House Divided.* Brookfield, CT: Millbrook, 1997.

Dudley, William, ed. *The Civil War: Opposing Viewpoints.* San Diego: Greenhaven Press, 1995.

Esposito, Vincent. *The West Point Atlas of the Civil War.* New York: Praeger, 1962.

Gay, Kathleen. *Civil War.* New York: Twenty-First Century Books, 1995.

Grabowski, Patricia. *Robert E. Lee: Confederate General.* New York: Chelsea House, 2001.

Hakim, Joy. *War, Terrible War.* New York: Oxford University Press, 1999.

Hewson, Martha. *Stonewall Jackson: Confederate General.* Philadelphia: Chelsea House, 2001.

Janis, Herbert. *The Civil War for Kids: A History with 21 Activities.* Chicago: Chicago Review Press, 1999.

Katz, William Loren. *An Album of the Civil War.* New York: Franklin Watts, 1974.

Lawson, Don. *The Union Story in the Civil War.* New York: Abelard-Schuman, 1977.

Levenson, Dorothy. *The First Book of the Confederacy.* New York: Franklin Watts, 1977.

McElfresh, Earl. *Maps and Mapmakers of the Civil War.* New York: Abrams, 1999.

Meltzer, Milton, ed. *Voices from the Civil War: A Documentary History of the Great American Conflict.* New York: Crowell, 1989.

Pflueger, Lynda. *Jeb Stuart: Confederate Cavalry General.* Springfield, NJ: Enslow, 1998.

Piggins, Carol Ann. *A Multicultural Portrait of the Civil War.* North Bellmore, NY: Marshall Cavendish, 1994.

Ransom, Candice F. *Children of the Civil War.* Minneapolis: Carolrhoda Books, 1998.

Remstein, Henna. *William Sherman: Union General.*
New York: Chelsea House, 2001.

Seidman, Rachel F. *The Civil War: A History in
Documents.* New York: Oxford University Press, 2001.

Stanchak, John E. *Visual Dictionary of the Civil War.*
New York: Dorling Kindersley, 2000.

Stefoff, Rebecca. *Abraham Lincoln.* Ada, OK: Garrett
Educational Corp., 1989.

Sullivan, George. *Mathew Brady: His Life and
Photographs.* New York: Cobblehill Books, 1994.

Time-Life Books. *Brother Against Brother: Time-Life
Books History of the Civil War.* New York: Prentice-Hall
Press, 1990.

Ward, Geoffrey. *The Civil War: An Illustrated History.* New
York: Knopf, 1990. (Based on the PBS documentary
series *The Civil War*, directed by Ken Burns)

Werstein, Irving. *The Many Faces of the Civil War.*
New York: Julian Messner, 1961.

Windrow, Martin. *The Civil War Rifleman.* New York:
Franklin Watts, 1985.

WEBSITES

www.homepages.dsu.edu/jankej/civilwar/civilwar.htm
Civil War Index Page, maintained by Dakota State
University, is a collection of links to online resources
in dozens of categories.

www.americancivilwar.com
American Civil War site includes timelines, battle maps,
documents such as the Emancipation Proclamation,
biographies of key figures, reading lists, and links to
other online sources.

ABOUT THE AUTHOR

Rebecca Stefoff is the author of many nonfiction books
for children and young adults. In Marshall Cavendish's
North American Historical Atlases, she draws upon her
interest in historical maps, life in different eras, and
military campaigns to tell the story of key events in
American history. Her account of the American Civil
War continues in *The Civil War: 1863–1865,* the com-
panion to this volume. Stefoff lives in Oregon, far from
the scenes of the Civil War, but she has visited many
Civil War sites. She appreciates the efforts of the
National Park Service, state and local historical soci-
eties, and other groups that work to preserve sites and
relics of the war so that they may continue to educate
and inspire us.

Index

WITHDRAWN

Desert Trip

by Barbara A. Steiner

Illustrations by Ronald Himler

Sierra Club Books for Children

San Francisco

The Sierra Club, founded in 1892 by John Muir, has devoted itself to the study and protection of the earth's scenic and ecological resources — mountains, wetlands, woodlands, wild shores and rivers, deserts and plains. The publishing program of the Sierra Club offers books to the public as a nonprofit educational service in the hope that they may enlarge the public's understanding of the Club's basic concerns. The point of view expressed in each book, however, does not necessarily represent that of the Club. The Sierra Club has some sixty chapters in the United States and Canada. For information about how you may participate in its programs to preserve wilderness and the quality of life, please address inquiries to Sierra Club, 85 Second Street, San Francisco, CA 94105, or visit our website at www.sierraclub.org.

First Edition

Library of Congress Cataloging-in-Publication Data

Steiner, Barbara A.
    Desert trip / by Barbara Steiner ; illustrated by Ronald Himler.
— 1st ed.
       p. cm.
    Summary: Relates the experiences of a young girl and her mother as they backpack in the desert where the child learns about the plants, animals, birds, and rock formations.
    ISBN 0-87156-581-1
    1. Deserts — Juvenile literature. [1. Deserts.] I. Himler, Ronald, ill. II. Title.
GB612.S735 1996
508.315'4 — dc20   95-24112

Art direction by Nanette Stevenson
Book and jacket design by Big Fish

Printed in Hong Kong
10 9 8 7 6 5 4 3 2

For my daughter, Rebecca,
and her daughter, Meghan.
Happy hiking!

— BAS

For Rich Genser

— RH

My mother and I are going backpacking in the desert canyonlands. As we drive the road to the beginning of the trail, I can see this is a magical place. All around us are huge rocks that look like castles against the desert sky.

At the parking lot where we'll leave our car behind, I struggle with my backpack. "I'm not sure I can carry this," I say, tugging on the shoulder straps.

Mother laughs and helps me. "Water *is* heavy. But we have to carry plenty, because we won't find much in the desert. When it does rain, the water soaks right into the sandy soil."

At last we're on our way. Now that the pack is on my back, it doesn't feel so heavy. We'll follow a trail up the mountain to a water hole and sleep outside overnight. Tomorrow we'll circle back to the car.

We walk over large, flat rocks that Mother calls slickrock. Wind and sand have polished the stone smooth. But it isn't really slick. My boots cling and climb the surface.

Mother says we're on a trail, but I can't see it. "What if we get lost?" I ask.

"Don't worry," she tells me. "I have a map, and I've hiked here lots of times. Besides, the trail is marked with small piles of rocks to show the way. See? This is called a cairn. We'll find others as we go along."

Soon I see another pile of rocks, and I feel better.

The sand gets deep, and my feet sink and slide. "Everything is so dry!" I say.

"Only plants that don't need much water can grow in the desert," Mother says. "Some plants don't bloom every year. They wait until there's a rain, and then they bloom almost overnight. But there must have been a lot of rain or snow this winter. The flowers are putting on quite a show."

Mother points to some tall stems covered with clusters of orange blossoms. Each one has a powder puff of yellow in the center. They're called globe mallow, she tells me.

Globe mallow

"And look at the old-man sagebrush," she says, pointing to some dusty silver-green branches that wave in the breeze. I touch them gently, and their stems feel like velvet.

I'm careful *not* to touch a spiny hedgehog cactus, even though each tiny stem bursts into a huge purple blossom.

I take a deep breath. "What's that spicy smell?"

"Cliff rose." Mother shows me the shrub, covered with creamy blossoms.

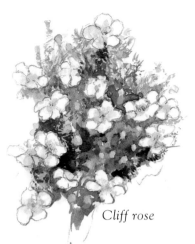

Cliff rose

"And smell this one."

"Strong," I say, wiggling my nose like a rabbit.

"It's yellow biscuit root. The native desert people — the Utes — dried and ground up the root to make flour. They used other desert plants to make medicine. Some plants out here are poisonous, though — so you should never eat one unless you know what it is."

Yellow biscuit root

Mother points to the soapweed yucca. "This root
lathers like soap. The native people wove twine and rope from the
leaves to make mats and sandals. And the buds are good to eat."

"It sure would be funny to go into the yard and pull up
some soap," I say. Mother and I laugh. "And I don't think I could
weave our shoes from leaves," she says.

As the trail heads upward again, I see scraggly trees. The wind has left them twisted and only a few feet tall.

"Look at those Utah juniper," Mother says, pulling off a small piece of the soft bark for me to touch. "A long time ago, Ute mothers used wads of this for baby diapers."

"The people didn't need a grocery store, did they?" I say. "They found everything they needed right here in the desert."

We walk up a dry stream bed and stop for lunch. "We should sit on those rocks," Mother says. "In the desert, a stream bed can flood suddenly."

"Even though it isn't raining?" I ask, looking at the sky.

"Yes, there could be a cloudburst up higher."

I choose a big, flat rock, take off my pack, and sit in the shade of a cottonwood tree. Mother digs around in her pack and soon pulls out our lunch — cheese and crackers, and peanut butter that we squeeze from a tube like toothpaste. For dessert, we eat dried apricots and nuts.

After I eat, I feel drowsy in the afternoon heat. The desert is the quietest place I have ever been. I lean back and doze. Then a canyon wren's trill runs down the scale like a piano exercise and echoes between the rocks.

Mother has been napping, too. "We'd better go," she says, yawning. "We need to reach our campground and water hole before dark."

We strap on our packs and start to walk again. Our trail leads up between the canyon walls. The rocks above us look to me like giant hamburgers with black mustard oozing over the buns. Some of the canyon walls are also stained. The black stuff is called desert varnish, Mother tells me. Native people scraped through the varnish to make pictures called petroglyphs.

Following the stream bed, we climb up slickrock that looks rippled and wavy. Mother helps me over the steep part. Far, far up, towering over us, is a sandstone arch.

"Water, wind, and sand carved that out over many, many years," Mother says. "The softer rock that was in the hole got worn away, and only the harder rock was left to form the arch."

As we hike higher and higher, I begin to see many things in the distant rocks. I see elephants, dinosaurs, and whales. There are huge mushrooms and gnomes. A turtle balances on a pointed rock, and a gigantic teapot looks ready to pour.

The sun sinks low in the sky as we reach our camp. We take off our packs and climb down some rocks. *Drip, drip, drip.* Under a low-hanging rock is a pool of water. It looks so cool and refreshing! We fill our bottles.

"Can I wade? Can I wiggle my toes in the pool?"

"Better not," says Mother. "We should leave the water clean for other hikers."

I explore and find several large, flat rocks. In one, there's a hole filled with water. "Oh, look! Tadpoles!"

"They probably belong to a spadefoot toad. When there's a big rain, the toad comes out of her sleeping place in the sand and lays her eggs. The tadpoles have to hatch and grow quickly, before the water dries up."

I check to make sure there aren't any tadpoles in my water bottle. Mother puts some drops in it to make it safe to drink. Then the water tastes like a swimming pool, so I stir in lemonade powder.

When it's time for dinner, we mix dried stew with water and cook it on a tiny stove that Mother has brought along in her pack. In my Sierra cup, I stir chocolate pudding mix with water until it's smooth and creamy. It tastes so good, I lick my spoon and cup so I don't miss a single drop.

The desert gets cold at night, so we build a small fire of dead juniper wood that we find lying on the ground. A tiny wisp of smoke rises into the dark sky. The smell reminds me of a cozy winter night.

I lie still near the fire, listening. The crackling sound of the flames keeps me company. A bat whirs by and dips into the water hole for a drink. Mother is sitting close by, looking up at the night sky.

I look up, too. I've never seen this many stars in the city. Here, I can't look at any piece of sky without seeing a star.

I plan to watch the fire burn down, but I fall asleep. When I open my eyes again, the sun has painted the red rocks gold. A mourning dove calls, *coo-coo, coo-coo.* The ravens squawk and scream as they chase across the empty sky. Cottonwood trees whisper in the soft breeze. Close by, on a rock, sits a cottontail rabbit. She doesn't see me watching as she washes her face like a cat.

We eat our breakfast of granola bars, dried apples, and powdered orange juice mixed with water. I roll up my sleeping bag and fasten it on my pack. We scatter the coals of our fire and leave our camp so clean that no one will know we were here.

Up and up we hike in the cool, clean morning air. Then we drop down between canyon walls, through narrow passageways, across slickrock ledges. I see so many secret playhouse places.

Some passageways are so narrow, I'm afraid I'll get stuck. I turn sideways and tiptoe so I can squeeze through. I pull and tug and finally pop out like a cork from a bottle. Mother laughs as I catch my balance again.

As we walk on, the only sound I hear is our boots crunching on the sandy trail. Up and over the slickrock we climb again. And suddenly, we're back at the parking lot where we left our car.

I feel sad to leave. Sad to hear car engines instead of the crunch of boots. Sad to hear the voices of people instead of the trill of the canyon wren. Sad to smell car fumes instead of spicy cliff rose.

Mother looks at my face and knows how I feel. "I feel the same way," she says quietly, putting her arm around me. "But the desert is like an old friend. It'll wait patiently for us until we come back again."

"Goodbye, old friend," I whisper.